Isaac Jenkinson Frazee, publisher Blade Printing Co.

Nahda

a Story of Spanish-American Life

Isaac Jenkinson Frazee, publisher Blade Printing Co.

Nahda

a Story of Spanish-American Life

ISBN/EAN: 9783743303676

Manufactured in Europe, USA, Canada, Australia, Japa

Cover: Foto ©ninafisch / pixelio.de

Manufactured and distributed by brebook publishing software
(www.brebook.com)

Isaac Jenkinson Frazee, publisher Blade Printing Co.

Nahda

NAHDA

A Story of Spanish- American Life ❧ ❧ ❧

THE paper-cutter on the cover of this little pastoral is a fragment of one of the old beams (11x13 inches and nearly 30 feet in length), from the San Luis Rey Mission, founded June 13, 1798. Tradition tells us this beam was hewn from the forest of Palomar Mountain, where it was sprinkled with holy water, placed on the shoulders of faithful Indians, and not allowed to touch the ground until the sacred mission site, twenty-five miles distant, was reached, relays of burden-bearers being stationed along the route to relieve their weary brethren. Some time ago, the Author, wishing to preserve one of these old beams, purchased it from Padre O'Keefe for the hall-way of Warland Tower, and this souvenir is a fragment of the same. The book-mark is a piece of the mission ceiling which was cast aside at the restoration some time ago.

Isaac Jenkinson - Frazer

Moosa Calif

ERRATA.

Page 20, the fourth line should read,
> "Kingly fruit for wayside beggar".

Page 21, the fourth line should read,
> "Cradle of the Spring-time flowers".

Page 32, the eleventh line should read,
> "In the one who soon brought ruin".

Page 32, the twentieth line should read,
> "We would roam the fields together".

With compliments of
Author

Warland Tower
Dec 10 1898

1798

S.R

1898

Moosa Cal. Dec. 10
1898

Dear Sir:

I send you under separate cover a copy of Wahda — which has become almost "extinct", in case you received in classifying the fossil. Please let me know what kind of a thing it is, to exhibit

"To the quaint old royal mission,
Wrapt in half-forgotten memories."

NAHDA

A Story of
Spanish-American Life

BY

ISAAC JENKINSON-FRAZEE

With Illustrations by the Author

OCEANSIDE, CAL.:
THE BLADE PRINTING CO.
1898

This little volume is affectionately dedicated to the good wife who shared with me the deprivations as well as pleasures of ranching

"'Mong the hills of Casa Loma"

—THE AUTHOR

NAHDA

CHAPTER I.

'Mong the hills of Casa Loma,
Where the wild bee sips the honey
From the dewy lips of sages,
Dwelt a maiden, with her father
Pedro Gomez, the sheep-herder.
When her eyes first ope'd to sunlight,
Life and Death met at her cradle:
Death smoothed out a mother's pillow—
Life found there a little orphan;
One so little, that they called her,
Half in pity, half derision—
Little "Nahda",* which translated
From the Spanish, means but "nothing".
Like a shepherd, whose long seeking,
Finds a lost lamb in the thicket,
Finds a ewe-lamb without mother;
So old Pedro hid his lambkin
With his sorrow, in his bosom.

* The Author has taken the liberty to change the
spelling of the Spanish word "Nada", pronounced Natha,
to "Nahda", the local pronunciation.

And a milk-goat, white as lilies,
Was half mother to the orphan;
Learned to love the little foundling,
Bleat and cry for little Nahda
As she would for her own offspring.
Unused hearts like locks, grow rusty;
All in vain we seek an entrance
Till we find the key of Sorrow.
Thus it was with Pedro Gomez,
And the love he bore his helpmate.
True, that love could ne'er be doubted;
Yet 'twas love's procrastination,
Kind words left until the morrow—
At her death, the morrow came.
She had gained her stoic patience
From her brave old Indian mother,
While a trusting faith was given
As her own paternal blessing,
For Don ——— of Pala Mission
Was indeed her very father;
And 'twas in the holy shadow
Of that Mission's quaint old belfry,
She found rest from all her burdens.
Pedro took his little burden
In his strong arms to his bosom,
Wept o'er it, his tears of penance,
Tears o'er Love's lost golden moments;
And 'tis well—for tears of sorrow
Prove our hearts are homes of angels,
Who, though transient guests, will linger

Seeking shelter in the portals.
Opened by the key of sorrow,
Angel feet may find an entrance
To a spacious, garnished chamber,
Fit home for that Man of Sorrows,
He who wept at tomb of Lazarus.

CHAPTER II.

Sadly to his home returning,
To the little thatched adobe,
Pedro found no kiss of welcome,
No dear word of happy greeting;
And the blossoms in her garden—
Flowers she had watched and cared for,
Watered through the long dry summer;
Hollyhocks and bright geraniums,
Violets and morning-glories,
Four-o'clocks and gay nasturtiums,
Golden pansies, golden poppies,
And the white rose on the trellis—
All with dew-drops seemed to glisten,
'Twas the tears upon his eyelids.
In the room all hope had vanished;
Through the little western window
Faded out the day in darkness,
And the crucifix in the corner
Caught the only gleam of sunlight.
'Twas the sign of Hope in darkness;
And the first time, since in childhood
He had knelt at knee of Mother,
Pedro Gomez found in prayer
Consolation for his sorrow.

As in death the aloe bloometh,
From that hour a new life opened;
And his last days were his best days.
Pedro's love grew warm and tender
For the babe within his bosom,
And in after years grew dearer,
As care leads to love's fruition.
Nahda thrived in his protection
As a wild flower 'neath an oak tree,
And her first days were all sunshine,
As bright morn precedes dark nightfall.
Slipped away the flying moments
Shod with tinkling golden sandals.
And the music of tame wild-birds
Taught her how to sing of Nature,
Trill of mocking-bird and linnet,
Pipe of tufted quail in thicket,
Liquid notes of lark in upland;
Drowsy hum of brown bees hunting
For the flower's hidden treasure;
Tinkle, tankle of the goat-bells,
And the bleating of the lambkins
Gamboling on the grassy hill-slope,
In the eve as they came homeward;
And the stories Pedro told her
As he swung her little hammock
When the toil of day was ended.
Told her of his dear Italia,
Of the grand, old picture galleries
Where the masters speak, tho' silent;

Of the palace halls and ruins
Near his mother's humble cottage;
Of his father's deeds of valor
On the Spanish field of battle,
How his lost cause drove in exile
Him and his small band of follow'rs;
How he sought a home in Italy,
Married there a peasant maiden,
One who knew but Want and Beauty,
Nothing but a straggling minstrel
Singing songs and making sunshine;
How he was their only offspring,
Spoiled and spanked as was convenient;
How he loved to hear her singing
As she worked within her garden,
And oft tried to imitate her
With his feeble childish lispings;
How his father painted frescoes
In the little village chapel,
Haloed saints and flying cherubs
In bewildering confusion.
Then the plague swept o'er the country
Striking down its helpless victims;
Claimed his parents as a ransom
For the freedom of their offspring.
And he taught her all the old songs
Written in his book of mem'ry,
Peasant songs of dear Italia,
War songs sung by his old father;
And the weird hymns and chantings

12

Of his own neglected helpmate.
Taught her how to play the mandolin;
And before she knew her letters,
She could sing his songs and play them;
Learned to sketch the scenes around her,
As one born to Art by Nature.

CHAPTER III.

Once there came a straggling artist
To the hills of Casa Loma,
Seeking for the subtile mys'try
Of their ever changing colors;
Of their half-tones and their shadows
Weaving veils of hazy distance
O'er the drowsy, dreamy landscape.
All in vain, he found his painting
Feeble grasps of helpless fingers
Reaching, as a child, for rainbows;
Yet he loved the scenes as fondly
As we love forbidden pleasures.
Loved to watch the sunset's splendor
Steal along the yellow hillsides,
Filling all the vale with crimson,
As tho' Nature's golden chalice
Brimmed with rosy wine of day dreams,
Vintage of bright hours' fruition.
Loved the grand, old, kingly mountains
Clad, as mete, in royal purple,
With their capes of snowy ermine,
And their golden crowns of sunset.
Loved to watch the sea-fog stealing,
As white spirits of the ocean,

Thro' the marsh lands in the moonlight;
Or to find, before the sunrise,
Inland sea o'er hidden valley;
Hilltops rising from the white mists,
Isles of gold in seas of silver,
Soon to vanish with day's coming,
Shrinking from the sunlight sceptres
As though Moses' rod passed o'er them.
But the hills to him were dearest,
Warm breasts of his first love, Nature,
Throbbing with her hidden secrets
Only told to favored lovers.
Those who rest upon her bosom
List'ning to each quick'ning heart beat,
Spellbound, captive to its music.
Where the corredor del camino *
Moans its plaintive, dove-like love song:
And the huitacoche † answers
From the distant sumac thicket,
His wee, sombre-coated bosom,
Throbbing with wierd echo-music,
Like the answering strains of harp strings;
Where wheat sparrows tell their secrets
In the sweetest trilling love songs;
Where the titmouse swings her hammock,
Formed like urn of woven silver,
Hanging from the pending branches

   * During the mating season the corredor del
camino, or road runner, sings a love song much
resembling the moaning of a dove.

   † Huitacoche. Indian name for song thrush.

15

To and fro like swinging censer,
Wafting lullabies to heaven;
Where lithe lizards, clad in armor
Of bright, iridescent colors,
Shimmer in the mellow sunlight,
Half asleep on lichen cushions.
E'en the whole land seems to slumber,
Wrapped in hazy folds of dream lace;
And the brown bees 'mong the poppies
Half forget their busy errands,
And, like idle, tippling minstrels,
Hum their drowsy, reeling measures.
Dreamy hills! fit place for dreaming—
Hills of sleep, this dreamer called them,
For here sleeps the Sphinx of Slumber, *
Hewn from out the solid syenite
By the mighty hand of Nature;
Lulled to sleep by foamy billows
Breaking on the stony seashore;
Dreaming of Creation's morning
When he first was bound in slumber.
Here this artist found contentment
Safe within the Sphinx's shadow;
And no wonder that long after,
When his lot was cast in turmoil
Of a city's ceaseless striving,
He should long for peace and quiet
Here within the arms of Nature,

* El Moro from the south resembles a sleeping
giant, and is known as the Sphinx of Slumber.

16

She who always bade him welcome
With her tawny arms wide open
To receive her heartsick lover,
Like a prodigal returning
From Art's husks or drunken banquet.
Many days was he aweary
Serving Art's capricious bidding,
Provided by the goad of hunger,
Hours of days for night's short pittance,
Pittance of Art's smiles and kisses,
Sipping dream-draughts from her chalice,
Rosy wine of subtile poison.
After ceaseless toil and hunger,
After death's fires brightly kindled,
Hectic flames on cheeks long careworn,
Came she then as tho' in pity
Sippings of success to offer;
But the tired hand dropped helpless
As the long sought cup she proffered.
Then Love found him by the wayside,
Pointed out a hopeful future,
Led him into paths of sunshine
Where a little, blue-eyed maiden
Through her golden curls peeped shyly;
Half in jest and half in earnest,
Gave our dreamer Hope's bright blossoms
Plucked from Youth's enchanting by-way.
But the frosts of Doubt oft blighted
Leaf and bloom of Hope's bright blossom,
Joy and pain by Fate compounded

Into life's one sweetest potion;
Honeyed nectar steeped in wormwood,
Fit draught for the lips of angels,
Cursed dregs for the tongues of demons.
Dreamer's heart, in disappointment,
Hastened to the arms of Nature;
Tossed upon her tawny bosom.
Hypocrite! love for her feigning,
When his heart was all another's—
One who heard of his sad illness,
Left her city home of comfort,
Cast aside Pride's flaunting mantle,
Donned habiliments of Mercy.
And o'er thousand miles of myst'ry
Sped she on, by Love's hand guided,
To his bedside and her bridal.
Heart and hand are tender nurses;
Hands and hearts, when joined together,
Turn life's shadows into sunshine.
Stood they there before the curate
On a rug by her hands fashioned,
Woven with her tears and prayers
For this, their one happiest moment.
She clad in soft, creamy satin,
And the flowers on her bosom
Were the fragrant elder-blossoms.
Thus it was that ever after
He loved them the best of flowers.
From the creamy elder-blossom
Fruit of liquid nectar ripens,

" 'Mong the hills of Casa Loma."

Dainty flavor of sweetwaters
Blended with the tart of currants;
White pearls crystalized in honey,
Kindly fruit for wayside beggar.
And as from the sterile soil
Elder-bloom to sweet fruit ripens,
So the fragrance of these flowers
Cast a spell of peaceful blessing
O'er their cozy little cottage,
In the "City of the Angels",
Which indeed to them was Heaven,
Heaven of Love 'mong those who loved them.

* * * * * * * * * * *

Then again Death's flames grew brighter
On the wan cheek, burning slowly
As though suffering stirred the embers;
So they left the little studio,
And among the pine-clad mountains
Sought the higher air, balm laden.
From the mountains to the foothills,
Thus like one, who, lost and wand'ring,
Finds his footstops circling backward,
Guided by a hand mysterious.
E'en it seems a law of Heaven,
Written in the book of Nature,
Circles hold the power of progress.
Every morn the earth returneth
To the trysting place of sunshine;
Planets move in God drawn circles,
Man returns to his Creator;

And the end finds the beginning.
Spirit seeking after spirit,
Dust to dust always returning;
Cradle to the Spring-time flowers
Coffin Autumn's scattered petals.
In these seeming aimless wand'rings
Fortune often guides our footsteps;
And 'twas thus these circling pilgrims
Came at last to Casa Loma;
Pitched their tent in hope and sunshine.
Soon a little redwood cabin
Peeped from out the vines and shrubbery.

*   *   *   *   *   *   *   *   *   *   *

And when next the elders blossomed
Came a rarer, fairer flower,
By the hand of Heaven given
As a blessing to their hearth-stone,
Came a man-child, full of promise,
Good of form and fair of feature;
Eyes, as blue as Eden pansies
Ringlets as the gold of Ophir.
Seemed as tho' two lovers hunting,
Found a tiny Cupid sleeping;
And in love made wee Love captive,
Who in turn bound fast his captors
With the golden links of child-love.
Bright his curl-crown shone upon him,
Bright his future beamed with promise,
And 'twas thus they called him Clarance,
Clarence, meaning the illustrious,

21

Name born of their great hopes for him,
Of their heart hope for his future.
Happy are the hearts which linger
In the path where child-love bloometh.
Sped too soon the toddling footsteps,
Through the flow'ry maze of childhood,
To the bright fields of Youth's morning
Where our little Spanish maiden
Led her lambkins 'mong the poppies;
And he loved the little Nahda.
Chased they butterflies together,
Hunted bird's nests in the heather,
Wove wreaths of the golden poppies
For the dear, old, white goat mother,
Nahda's faithful foster-mother.
Nahda sketched the little lambkins
With the cunning hand of genius—
Genius taught by good Dame Nature—
And 'twas she who first awakened
In the sleeping heart of Clarence
All the art-love lying dormant,
Waiting for the kiss of Springtime;
And 'twas Clarence who led Nahda,
Proud, in triumph for her genius,
To his father's open atelier,
There to gain his admiration
And the blessing of his teaching.
From that hour her life expanded

In the new surroundings offered,
And she shared alike with Clarence
All the father's proud affection;
Came and went as impulse led her,
To the old or to the new home.
How her art bloomed forth in promise!
How her heart with home-love blossomed!
Lightly danced the happy hours
To the rippling strains of laughter.
O'er the hills with Pedro herding,
O'er the hills with Clarence sketching,
To the trysting place of twilight
On the summit of El Moro;
To where, guarding shady fastness,
Stands the grim, grey tower of Warland;
To Guajome's Spanish courtyard
With its wealth of orange blossoms;
To the quaint, old, royal Mission
Wrapt in half forgotten mem'ries;
To the ocean with its mys'try,
And its sullen stretch of sadness;
Or to heights of Palomar,
Where the pines sing Nature's anthems;
Hither, thither, where Fate beckoned,
Heedless of the coming morrow.
Nahda's genius bloomed in Clarence,
As his love within her blossomed.
'Tis the same old rule in love-lore,
Woman counts it gain in losing
Art and self for Love's rewarding.

23

And 'tis best so—Love that's drossless,
Standing flames of fiery passions,
Tarnished not by sordid fingers;
Bearing, through its daily usage,
Still the "kingly superscription"
Is mete payment for Life's losses.

Late one eve on old El Moro,
As the sun sank down in splendor
To his couch of golden turquoise,
Clarence told her of the sorrow
Breaking in his boyish bosom;
How the morrow brought their parting—
He to sail for Art and Future,
She to cheer his widowed mother
With a daughter's true devotion,
Till time called the foster brother
Back to home and love and loving.

CHAPTER IV.

Nahda knew naught of church dogmas,
Worshipped but the God of Nature;
Found His footprints 'mong the blossoms,
Heard His voice among the rushes,
Saw the tracings of His fingers
On the fern fronds in the canyon.
She had also heard the story
Of the "Babe within the manger",
And her young heart yearned in pity
O'er the cruel crucifixion.
From the two she drew this lesson,
"That to gain the Life Eternal
She must walk close to the Savior,
Thus would find the God of Nature";
Yet this love for God and Nature
Brought her little consolation
For the sorrow in her bosom.
God and Nature seemed to slumber
Through the long, dry days of summer;
Neither brought her word of comfort
For the hidden grief within her.
Turned she to her household duties,
Buried self in thought of others,
Smoothed the way for good old Pedro,

Gave a daughter's love and service
To the dear, kind foster-mother.
E'en the tawny hills she pitied,
Her helpless, thirsty, panting hills,
Athrob with palpitating heat,
Like brown deer weary from the chase.

"To Guajome's Spanish courtyard
With its wealth of orange blossoms."

CHAPTER V.

'Twas the time when booms were booming
That Joe Gifford grew ambitious,
And the Rancho del Camino—
Although many leagues containing—
Was too small for this young hopeful.
Had he not gained one and twenty,
And was he not his own master?
So he hied him to the city
Real estate to sell to "suckers";
Fitted up a nobby office,
Bright with tea-store green and scarlet,
And the paint was not through drying
Ere the "suckers" came by dozens,
Nibbling at the choice bait offered.
"Corner lots in charming Boomville,
Only eight miles from the courthouse,
Reached by proposed line of railway,
Where the proposed Southern College
And the proposed Hotel Eclat
Will propose to take in tourists,
(Take in "suckers", take in money);
In return will give 'em climate,
Give 'em health-restoring climate,
Give 'em stationary climate"—

That is, climate that won't climb it,
Nor won't lower 'till you want it;
Balmy climate of the tropics,
Climate for worn-out consumptives,
Climate which will cure the asthma,
Cure the mumps and rheumatism,
Cure, in fact, all ills and ailings;
Climate which will make you pious,
Climate which will make you wealthy,
Climate which is good for lying.
Give 'em views of sea and mountain,
Give 'em visions of the future,
Give 'em choice lots on the main street,
Lots which promise soon to double;
Lots of promises he gives 'em,
(True in one sense—not in grammar);
But the promise of more "suckers"
Sometimes makes the trade a bargain;
For the festive agent ponders
O'er the maxim and reads this wise,
"Do to others as you're done by."
Yet for invalids (so thoughtful)
Sub-divides up wildcat ranches
Into "to be" climate cities;
Land which truly is so worthless
Naught 'twill raise but suckers' shekels;
Lots so steep you have to stake 'em,
Or they'd slip into the canyon,
Where if you could plow a furrow
It at noon would cast a shadow.

Other lots out in tide water,
As if they'd got tired of waiting
For the Flume, and, being thirsty,
Slipped down hill and had to stay there;
For although their boast was climate
Yet they could not clim' it from there.
Gifford picked up eighty acres
On the railroad at the seaside;
Bought it for one thousand dollars—
Partly cash, but mostly promise—
From the shepherd, Pedro Gomez.
Pedro knew scant ways of trick'ry,
Held a promise as though sacred;
Gifford, wise in ways of cunning,
Weak in all true mental merit,
Paid each tardy, unpaid promise
With another brighter promise,
Till the glamour of great promise
Crowned his every act with promise,
Till this promising young fellow
Filled the air with glorious promise.
In his smile a rainbow fluttered,
At whose base the dupes dug often
For the pot of hidden treasure.
"Mira Mar" he called his purchase,
"Eye of the Sea", to blind their seeing;
Not the first time good old Spanish
Has by Greed been used for blinding,
As enticing bait to tourists
Seeking after things romantic,

For a promise full of promise.
Gifford's acres soon bore harvest
In a maze of whitened lot stakes;
At the corners in bright letters
Shone the name of street and alley—
"Victoria Place", "Boulevarde Royal",
"Elm Street","Pine Street","Windsor Terrace",
"Maple," "Market" "City Plaza"—
All so full of thrifty promise
That it spread in epidemic,
Till every seeker after promise
Had been stricken with the fever.
What cared they for perfect title
When half pay gave perfect pleasure,
Or an advance from some other
Kept the title full of promise?
Gifford shrewdly took advantage
Of each hastily made transaction
To salt down his ill got earnings
Into other hidden channels.
In the small spring at the roadside
Poured he sulphur, put in horse shoes,
Doctored it till taste and odor
Made it famous as a tonic.
And the band played in the Plaza,
Calling crowds to free lunch tables,
While in line the buyers waited
For their chance at speculation.
Pedro, in anticipation
Of the fruiting days of promise,

Mortgaged all the rich home acres
To secure Joe Gifford's venture,
And thus save himself and Nahda
Till Joe Gifford's promise ripened.
Generous Pedro, never doubting,
Did not feel the strands grow tighter,
As this human spider wove them
Back and forth across his doorway.
And 'twas thus he died, still trusting
In the one he had befriended,
In the one who ~~had~~ Soon brought ruin
To the home of Pedro Gomez.
In his illness called he Nahda,
"Nahda, Nahda, little lambkin,
Come thou here within my bosom
Where so often I have held thee.
Now I go to distant pastures,
Pastures full of Heavenly promise.
Oh! that thou might'st journey thither;
We would ~~walk~~ roam the fields together,
Find the long lost mother waiting
For her tardy love and lambkin."
Then delirious, called he to her,
Drew from out its secret hiding
A stiletto—keen as malice,
Gave it to his weeping daughter
Saying, "Take it, keep it, Nahda;
In the life of every woman
Comes a time when the stiletto
May take place of sire or brother

32

To avenge insulted honor.
Wolves grow daring at the lamb-fold,
When the tired shepherd sleepeth.
Let Clarence be thy foster-brother,
And be thou his mother's hand-maid;
And if in an hour of trouble,
Thou need one to shield, protect thee,
Seek thou, my good friend, Joe Gifford."

CHAPTER VI.

News of Clarence coming homeward
Brought again the tardy roses
To the cheek of Nahda Gomez.
On El Moro kept she vigil,
Watching for the passing steamer
That would bring again her lover
From Gate of Gold to Gate of Silver.

* * * * * * * * * * *

Just a grey speck on the ocean
With its trailing smoky streamer,
Creeping slowly, scarcely moving—
How her heart beat wild, impatient,
Fluttering with love-born pinions.
Brave is rustic love, impulsive,
Heedless of the World's approval,
Caring naught for laws of loving,
Guided, by Love's intuition.

* * * * * * * * * * *

Once again they roamed together
O'er the flow'ry hills of promise,
Hearts attuned to happy lark-song.
Clarence, though a man in stature,
Yet still kept within his bosom
All the boyish love for Nature,

All the tender love for Nahda.
Oft they journeyed to the mountains,
To the little Indian village
Where the Agua Caliente *
Pours its healing, thermal waters.
There they found an aged Indian—
Pablo, once a mighty chieftain—
Who, a seer among his people,
Told the Past, the Present, Future,
As it were a scroll before him;
Told of how past generations
Held these springs against invaders;
How the padres blessed these waters
As a gift unto their children;
How the cunning white man halted
At their brink, with compromises
For the rich leagues they had stolen;
How today the white man, spying.
Comes to seek these thermal waters,
And, ere many moons have vanished,
Will deprive them of their birthright.
Then a plaintive wail of anguish
Rose upon the desert stillness,
As a lost soul, in the darkness
Calling to the God of Mercy,
"Save us! Save us! Father, save us!
Save thy homeless, helpless children."
Nahda conned their folk-lore secrets

* The Indians living at these springs are known
as the Agua Caliente and at the present moment
white men are trying to drive them from their homes

For the willing ear of Clarence;
How the Agua Calientes
Have an old and weird legend—
Woven in a woof of fancy
By the weaver, Superstition—
How a chieftain's daughter, Deros,
Was forsaken by her lover,
Thrown aside as tattered garment,
As a garment worn and faded.
In the heart of every woman
Nests the cooing dove and eagle:
When the dove spreads forth her pinions
Naught remains but "bird of hatred,"
Screaming loud, demanding vengeance;
And 'tis thus that Deros follows
Every step of recreant lover,
Watching with an eye of vengeance,
Meting out just retribution:
Many other folk-lore lessons
Learned they from the lips of Pablo;
And the grand old Indian's spirit
Found an echo in the bosom
Of brave Nahda's savage nature.
How she longed to free this people
From the merc'less white man's thraldom.
Through her sympathy and birthright,
That half taint of Indian nature,
She became as Pablo's daughter,
As a priestess for his people;
And 'twas thus his hidden secrets

"To where, guarding shady fastness,
Stands the grim, grey Tower of Warland."
(Home of the Author.)

Found safe hiding in her bosom.
As of old the Egyptian priestess
Scattered myrrh on glowing embers,
And from out the rising vapors
Fashioned forms, of weird myst'ry;
So o'er hills, by sunset kindled,
Nature casts wild herbs, sweet-scented,
And from out the hazy heat-mist
Rise ethereal, subtile dream-forms;
Dream-forms, wherein Nature's children
Hear an answer from their mother.
The earth beneath and sky above them
Sharing each its hidden secret,
Spirit forms of rising vapor,
Whisperings of fragrant flowers,
Moanings of the winds about them,
And the silence of the stars—
All in praise to that Great Spirit
Who hath made them for his children.

* * * * * * * * * * *

Clarence found the long vacation
Short enough for love and loving;
And it was with greatest effort
Tore he from the arms of Nahda;
But full soon, fond Art's caresses
Wooed him to the heights of promise;
And yet oit from Paris' salons
Looked he back, with heartsick longing,
For the hills of Casa Loma,
And his little Spanish sweetheart.

From the twilight of his pictures
Beamed the tender eyes of Nahda.
Every fibre of his canvas
Seemed to breathe her very presence.
Wove he art and heart together,
Warp and woof so closely blended,
None could tell the one's beginning,
None could tell the other's ending.
Came her letters, bearing comfort,
Full of faith in his great future,
Full of love and love's true brav'ry;
Scantily hiding her heart-longing.
After while they came less frequent,
Soon no message came to cheer him
From his love across the water.
Still he wrote, but heard no tidings,
Still his heart called out in anguish;
Called in vain, for silence answered.
Paltry seemed the hard won medals,
Lonely grew the life about him;
For loneliest of all earth's places
Are loveless hearts where crowds assemble.

CHAPTER VII.

Tho' Joe Gifford brought sad ruin
To dead Pedro's little holdings—
Driving Nahda from her childhome—
Yet so sly this cunning villain,
Smooth of tongue and hypocritic,
Still he posed as her protector;
Blinded still the eyes of Nahda,
Wept with her o'er her misfortune,
In confidence told all his troubles,
Till her poor heart warmed with pity
For the sorrow in his bosom.
Little Nahda's trust grew greater,
As his meshes bound her tighter:
Told she him, her love for Clarence;
And he, smiling, gave false blessing,
While within his heart in secret
Hissed he curses on his rival,
Curses from his heart of passion;
Yet poor Nahda never doubted.
Was he not the soul of honor?
Came he not from the Vale of Virtue?
Where temptations prove abortive,
And the trusty maid and matron

40

Wade through blood to save their honor?
Was he not the people's chosen,
Chosen by his voting kinsmen
For a place of trust and honor?
Little knew she how he'd trampled
Every trust beneath his footsteps,
Every promise violated;
And how their own tax grown coffers
Had been squandered on his kinsmen,
Or been bartered for a foll'wing.
Trusting still imagined honor,
Shared she all her secrets with him;
And he gave her golden trinkets,
Each as link in passion's fetters.
Followed he as though her shadow,
Fawning o'er her as a spaniel,
Came and went at beck or bidding,
Ever ready for her errands;
Posted he each tender missive,
Brought he every precious message;
Till her love for Clarence blossomed
Into warm respect for Gifford.
Soon the letters were not posted,
Soon the prying eyes looked inward
Seeking for each hidden secret;
Building up, with stones of malice,
A foundation for his lying.
To the name of fair Belle Creighton—
Borrowed from a stolen message
Wherein Clarence wrote to Nahda

41

Of his cousin's coming nuptials—
Added he a startling story
Of the faithlessness of Clarence;
Carried it in ghoulish triumph
To the ears of little Nahda.
Pressed her hand upon the dagger,
Flashed her eye with burning anger,
At this insult to her lover.
Gifford, trembling, begged her mercy;
Wept, that he should bring such sorrow
To the heart he loved so dearly;
Offered her his consolation.
But she sprang, a tigress, from him
To her wanderings in the mountains;
Safe within El Moro's cavern
Hid she with her searing sorrow.

CHAPTER VIII.

Clarence cast aside his brushes,
Cast aside the dross of glory
For the lost gold of his loving,
For the treasure he had hidden
'Mong the hills of Casa Loma,
Wondering if aught had stolen
That, which seemed to him so precious.
Little knew he of the robber
Who had sought to steal and tarnish;
Little knew the lonely Nahda
How the cowardice of Gifford
Shrank from touching that rich treasure—
That pure, drossless gold of nature—
Through his fear of Nahda's dagger.
Hastened he across the water,
Storm-tossed in his soul and body,
Buffeted with doubts, misgivings;
Yearning for a hopeful message,
Dreading lest it bring him sorrow.

*   *   *   *   *   *   *   *   *   *   *

At the spring in Shadow Canyon
Found they Clarence Cooper dying,
Dying from its poisoned waters;
And Joe Giffords name was whispered,

Lip to ear by soft-voiced scandal.
On the summit of El Moro,
As 'twas mete for him who loved it,
He was buried at the twilight
'Mongst his scenes of inspiration.

CONCLUSION.

Deros, in El Moro's cavern,
With her grey head bowed in sorrow,
Sways her body, moaning, chanting:
"Down in a cold, dark grave
Where the slimy worm doth crawl,
Winding its length through the musty damp,
Where the drops of water fall,
Dripping, dripping in monotone,
Alone! Alone! Alone! Alone!
Hidden beneath the cold grey stone,
Forgotten! Alone! Alone! Alone! "
Clarence, waking from his stupor,
In the bowels of the mountain,
Hears and sees the aged Deros.
Deros points her trembling finger,
And, with voice of scorn, she hisses,
"Mortal from the land of living,
I am Deros, the Avenger.
He, who on a girl's heart tramples,
He, who blights a girl's affection,
From my hand receives no pity;
In my vengeance finds no mercy.
I have seen a poor girl wand'ring
O'er the hills of thorny cactus,

'Mong the briars in the canyon,
Wandering as if demented.
On her face was anguish written;
And her locks, which once were raven,
Now are white with snows of sorrow;
While within her throbbing bosom
Burns the impress of your footstep—
Nahda Gomez' heart is broken.

CLARENCE:

Be ye saint or be ye demon,
Tho' no mercy will be granted,
By the powers of light and darkness,
By my love for Nahda Gomez,
Tho' my life should be the forfeit,
Demon Deros, thou art lying!

DEROS:

Tho' my heart be barred to mercy,
Yet it opens wide to reason.
Swear ye by your love for Nahda,
When your heart is all another's?
When your marriage with Belle Creighton
Was but stopped by Death's intrusion?

CLARENCE:

Demon, is your eye so evil
It can see but sin, in mortal?
Else you might have read the sorrow
In my heart, with tear-drops written;
How I sought for Nahda Gomez,
But in vain was all my seeking.
When you read the hearts of mortals,

46

You should strive to read more careful;
Not mistake the love of kindred
For the marriage vows of true love—
This Belle Creighton is my cousin,
And her heart is all another's—
One she loves with my approval.
As a miser loves his money,
As a pagan loves his idol,
As a mother loves her first-born,
So my heart loves Nahda Gomez;
Yet I would not seek thy mercy
For, since lost is Nahda Gomez,
I defy the plagues of Hades."

Nahda's heart, half dead with sorrow,
Found in tears a long sought blessing,
As a thirsty land in summer
Finds new life in falling raindrops.
Fell the veil, her face disclosing,
Fell her grey head on his bosom;
Sobbing like a child forsaken,
Sobbed and moaned like distant water;
Pleading for his love and mercy,
Cringing, craving for his pardon.
Told him of her days of waiting,
Weeks and months for his returning;
How Joe Gifford, through his lying,
Caused her trusting heart to doubt him;
How she wandered to the mountains,
Sought a home among the Indians;

There she found the herb of slumber,
Made a draught to quench her mem'ry,
Seeking thus the Past to bury.
After hours of dreamless slumber,
To the living Past awakened,
Found she could not live without him,
Would return and seek his pity:
If not granted, would seek slumber,
Drink enough of the solution
To cause death—and thus forget him;
How she found him in the garden
Talking with the fair Belle Creighton,
Speaking of the coming nuptials;
And her hair turned white in anguish,
And the fires died in her bosom.
Then Hate whispered, "Love's departed;
Drive him from his golden castle,
From the heart of this Belle Creighton";
How she sought to make him slumber,
Thus forget his new allegiance;
Wake to love her as of olden.
So the little spring was poisoned,
And his mother found him lying,
Seeming dead, within the canyon;
How they did as he'd requested,
Buried him at hour of twilight
On the summit of El Moro;
How she hid and watched them leaving,
Then worked fast to gain his body,
Seeking thus to steal affection,

Knowing, after hours of sleeping,
He would surely soon awaken.
All of this and more she told him,
Sobbing, told and asked for mercy.
Thro' her snowy hair of sorrow
Ran the tears of his forgiveness;
Kissing, promised none should ever
Share the secret of his dying.
Then she led him out the cavern,
And adown the winding pathway
Where the little funeral cortege
Passed, not many hours before them.
Closer to his heart he drew her,
Fearing she might vanish from him;
Whispered words of love and comfort—
Still she sobbed and prayed in silence,
Thanking God for all His goodness,
Worshiping thro' her own idol.
Down the narrow, winding pathway,
Through the silv'ry morning moonlight,
On and on toward Casa Loma,
Through the maze of sage and buckwheat,
Pressed their eager, hopeful footsteps.

THE END.

www.ingramcontent.com/pod-product-compliance
Lightning Source LLC
Chambersburg PA
CBHW022039080426
42733CB00007B/894